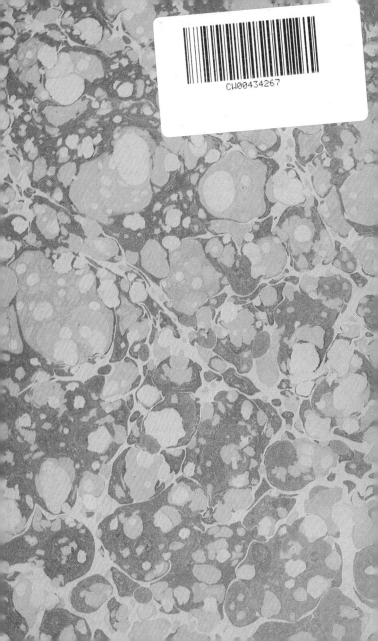

THE ILLUSTRATED POETS

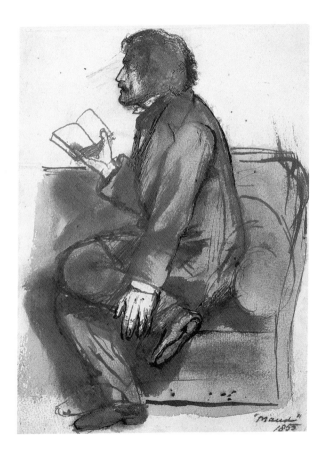

"Maud"
1855

THE ILLUSTRATED POETS

Alfred Lord Tennyson

Selected and with an introduction
by Geoffrey Moore

AURUM PRESS

First published 1994 by Aurum Press Ltd,
25 Bedford Avenue, London WC1B 3AT
Selection and introduction copyright © 1994 by Geoffrey Moore

A catalogue record of this book is available from the British Library.

ISBN 1 85410 345 8

2 4 6 8 10 9 7 5 3 1
1995 1997 1998 1996 1994

Picture research by Juliet Brightmore
Printed in Hong Kong by Imago

CONTENTS

INTRODUCTION

Alfred Tennyson was born on August 6, 1809, in the Rectory of Somersby, Lincolnshire. His father, Dr George Clayton Tennyson, was a man of considerable learning and literary sensibility but prone to bouts of depression and violent drunkenness, having been disinherited, forced into the Church, and generally treated as a nincompoop by his own father, the powerful and tyrannical 'Old Man of the Wolds'.

The tumultuous Somersby household, with its eleven children, was at once good and bad for the young Alfred – good in that, after a period at Louth Grammar School, he was educated by his father who encouraged him in his natural inclination to write, and bad in that constant quarrels and upheavals fuelled the tendency toward melancholia which he had inherited.

When Tennyson entered Trinity College, Cambridge, his poetic prowess had already been trumpeted by his friends and relations. The fact that – in addition to his genuine talent – he was Byronically handsome, with his dark, romantic, shaggy head and powerful body, did nothing to harm his reputation. Many of his friends, including Arthur Hallam, son of the historian Henry Hallam, were members of a group known as the 'Apostles', which met to discuss contemporary ethical and religious problems. For them Tennyson was not only a great poet but the voice of his generation.

Tennyson's friendship with Hallam was a major event in his life. Hallam, who was also a poet, had not only a clear-eyed perception of the nature of his friend's genius, but in addition such a love, wholeheartedly

returned, that his father objected to the amatory tone of several of his son's poems and letters. Hallam's death in 1833 plunged Tennyson into a severe depression, particularly since it followed hard on the unfavourable reception of *Poems, Chiefly Lyrical*, in 1830, and vitriolic notices of *Poems* (1832), which included 'The Lotos-Eaters' and 'The Lady of Shalott'.

The postponement of Tennyson's marriage to Emily Sellwood, whom he had first met in 1830 and was officially engaged to in 1838, is usually said to have been for financial reasons, but the award in 1845 of a Civil List pension of £200 a year certainly eased his burden. When his moving series of elegies on his friend's death was finally published as *In Memoriam* in 1850, perhaps he felt free. 1850 was, in fact, an *annus mirabilis* for Tennyson. *In Memoriam* received not only popular acclaim but also the approval of Prince Albert; Tennyson was appointed to succeed Wordsworth as Poet Laureate; and, at the age of forty-one, he married Emily. Three years later the couple moved to the Isle of Wight, where they brought up their two sons.

In 1842 Tennyson published a collection of *Poems*, which included 'Ulysses'. *The Princess*, considerably in advance of its time (1847), had as its subject the role of women in society. Maud (1855) was one of Tennyson's favourites, and he loved to read it aloud. He described it as 'the history of a morbid poetic soul raised to a pure and holy love ... driven into madness by the loss of her whom he has loved'. *Idylls of the King* (1859) sold ten thousand copies in its first week and Tennyson began preparing a new editon which he sent to Queen Victoria in 1862. He was invited to Osborne and learned how the Queen had drawn consolation for Prince Albert's death from *In Memoriam*. Everything he

did except – to his disappointment – his plays, was received with acclaim. A stream of eminent persons – Garibaldi, Turgenev, Darwin, Huxley – came to visit him at Farringford. He brought out Enoch Arden in 1864, completed *Idylls of the King* with *The Holy Grail* in 1869, and in his old age continued to produce.

Tennyson's achievement lay in interpreting the Victorian age to itself. He used his subjects, historical, mythological or scientific, in order to express opinions which provoked yet satisfied his readers. The essence of his poetic genius – as Hallam defined it when Tennyson was still in his early twenties – lay in his 'luxuriance of imagination', in his 'vivid, picturesque delineation of objects', and in 'the variety of his lyrical measures and exquisite modulation of harmonious words'.

This is exactly it. T.S. Eliot considered Tennyson had 'the finest ear of any poet since Milton'. But it is more than a question of 'ear'. Tennyson possessed, in addition, something of that quality of 'auditory imagination', which works, Eliot said, not through sound only or meaning only but through a combination of both, causing a reverberation of the soul that goes deep into the past of the language.

In 1883 Tennyson accepted the peerage which he had declined several times before. In 1889 he had a premonition of death which caused him to write 'Crossing the Bar'. He did not die, however, until October 6, 1892, with his family around him and a volume of Shakespeare open to his hand. He was buried in Westminster Abbey.

GEOFFREY MOORE

The Lady of Shalott

PART I

On either side the river lie
Long fields of barley and of rye,
That clothe the wold and meet the
    sky;
And thro' the field the road runs by
    To many-tower'd Camelot;
And up and down the people go,
Gazing where the lilies blow
Round an island there below,
    The island of Shalott.

Willows whiten, aspens quiver,
Little breezes dusk and shiver
Thro' the wave that runs for ever
By the island in the river
    Flowing down to Camelot.
Four gray walls, and four gray towers,
Overlook a space of flowers,
And the silent isle imbowers
    The Lady of Shalott.

By the margin, willow-veil'd,
Slide the heavy barges trail'd
By slow horses; and unhail'd
The shallop flitteth silken-sail'd
    Skimming down to Camelot:
But who hath seen her wave her hand?
Or at the casement seen her stand?
Or is she known in all the land,
    The Lady of Shalott?

Only reapers, reaping early
In among the bearded barley,
Hear a song that echoes cheerly
From the river winding clearly,
    Down to tower'd Camelot:
And by the moon the reaper weary,
Piling sheaves in uplands airy,
Listening, whispers, ''Tis the fairy
    Lady of Shalott.'

The Lotos-Eaters

CHORIC SONG

I

There is sweet music here that softer falls
Than petals from blown roses on the grass,
Or night-dews on still waters between walls
Of shadowy granite, in a gleaming pass;
Music that gentlier on the spirit lies,
Than tir'd eyelids upon tir'd eyes;
Music that brings sweet sleep down from the bliss-
    ful skies.
Here are cool mosses deep,
And thro' the moss the ivies creep,
And in the stream the long-leaved flowers weep,
And from the craggy ledge the poppy hangs in sleep.

II

Why are we weigh'd upon with heaviness
And utterly consumed with sharp distress,
While all things else have rest from weariness?
All things have rest: why should we toil alone,
We only toil, who are the first of things,
And make perpetual moan,
Still from one sorrow to another thrown:
Nor ever fold our wings,
And cease from wanderings,
Nor steep our brows in slumber's holy balm;
Nor harken what the inner spirit sings,
'There is no joy but calm!'
Why should we only toil, the roof and crown of
    things?

III

Lo! in the middle of the wood,
The folded leaf is woo'd from out the bud

With winds upon the branch, and there
Grows green and broad, and takes no care,
Sun-steep'd at noon, and in the moon
Nightly dew-fed; and turning yellow
Falls, and floats adown the air.
Lo! sweeten'd with the summer light,
The full-juiced apple, waxing over-mellow,
Drops in a silent autumn night.
All its allotted length of days,
The flower ripens in its place,
Ripens and fades, and falls, and hath no toil,
Fast-rooted in the fruitful soil.

IV

Hateful is the dark-blue sky,
Vaulted o'er the dark-blue sea.
Death is the end of life; ah, why
Should life all labour be?
Let us alone. Time driveth onward fast,
And in a little while our lips are dumb.
Let us alone. What is it that will last?
All things are taken from us, and become
Portions and parcels of the dreadful Past.
Let us alone. What pleasure can we have
To war with evil? Is there any peace
In ever climbing up the climbing wave?
All things have rest, and ripen toward the grave
In silence; ripen, fall and cease:
Give us long rest or death, dark death, or dreamful
     ease.

V

How sweet it were, hearing the downward stream,
With half-shut eyes ever to seem
Falling asleep in a half-dream!

To dream and dream, like yonder amber light,
Which will not leave the myrrh-bush on the
      height;
To hear each other's whisper'd speech;
Eating the Lotos day by day,
To watch the crisping ripples on the beach,
And tender curving lines of creamy spray;
To lend our hearts and spirits wholly
To the influence of mild-minded melancholy;
To muse and brood and live again in memory,
With those old faces of our infancy
Heap'd over with a mound of grass,
Two handfuls of white dust, shut in an urn of brass!

VI

Dear is the memory of our wedded lives,
And dear the last embraces of our wives
And their warm tears: but all hath suffer'd change:
For surely now our household hearths are cold:
Our sons inherit us: our looks are strange:
And we should come like ghosts to trouble joy.
Or else the island princes over-bold
Have eat our substance, and the minstrel sings
Before them of the ten years' war in Troy,
And our great deeds, as half-forgotten things.
Is there confusion in the little isle?
Let what is broken so remain.
The Gods are hard to reconcile:
'Tis hard to settle order once again.
There *is* confusion worse than death,
Trouble on trouble, pain on pain,
Long labour unto aged breath,
Sore task to hearts worn out by many wars
And eyes grown dim with gazing on the pilot-stars.

VII

But, propt on beds of amaranth and moly,
How sweet (while warm airs lull us, blowing
    lowly)
With half-dropt eyelid still,
Beneath a heaven dark and holy,
To watch the long bright river drawing slowly
His waters from the purple hill –
To hear the dewy echoes calling
From cave to cave thro' the thick-twined vine –
To watch the emerald-colour'd water falling
Thro' many a wov'n acanthus-wreath divine!
Only to hear and see the far-off sparkling brine,
Only to hear were sweet, stretch'd out beneath the
    pine.

VIII

The Lotos blooms below the barren peak:
The Lotos blows by every winding creek:
All day the wind breathes low with mellower tone:
Thro' every hollow cave and alley lone
Round and round the spicy downs the yellow
    Lotos-dust is blown.
We have had enough of action, and of motion we,
Roll'd to starboard, roll'd to larboard, when the
    surge was seething free,
Where the wallowing monster spouted his foam-
    fountains in the sea.
Let us swear an oath, and keep it with an equal
    mind,
In the hollow Lotos-land to live and lie reclined
On the hills like Gods together, careless of
    mankind.
For they lie beside their nectar, and the bolts are
    hurl'd

Far below them in the valleys, and the clouds are
    lightly curl'd
Round their golden houses, girdled with the
    gleaming world:
Where they smile in secret, looking over wasted
    lands,
Blight and famine, plague and earthquake, roaring
    deeps and fiery sands,
Clanging fights, and flaming towns, and sinking
    ships, and praying hands.
But they smile, they find a music centred in a
    doleful song
Steaming up, a lamentation and an ancient tale of
    wrong,
Like a tale of little meaning tho' the words are
    strong;
Chanted from an ill-used race of men that cleave
    the soil,
Sow the seed, and reap the harvest with enduring
    toil,
Storing yearly little dues of wheat, and wine and
    oil;
Till they perish and they suffer – some, 'tis
    whisper'd – down in hell
Suffer endless anguish, others in Elysian valleys
    dwell,
Resting weary limbs at last on beds of asphodel.
Surely, surely, slumber is more sweet than toil, the
    shore
Than labour in the deep mid-ocean, wind and wave
    and oar;
Oh rest ye, brother mariners, we will not wander
    more.

Morte d'Arthur

So all day long the noise of battle roll'd
Among the mountains by the winter sea;
Until King Arthur's table, man by man,
Had fallen in Lyonnesse about their Lord,
King Arthur: then, because his wound was deep,
The bold Sir Bedivere uplifted him,
Sir Bedivere, the last of all his knights,
And bore him to a chapel nigh the field,
A broken chancel with a broken cross,
That stood on a dark strait of barren land.
On one side lay the Ocean, and on one
Lay a great water, and the moon was full.
Then spake King Arthur to Sir Bedivere:
'The sequel of to-day unsolders all
The goodliest fellowship of famous knights
Whereof this world holds record. Such a sleep
They sleep – the men I loved. I think that we
Shall never more, at any future time,
Delight our souls with talk of knightly deeds,
Walking about the gardens and the halls
Of Camelot, as in the days that were.
I perish by this people which I made, –
Tho' Merlin sware that I should come again
To rule once more – but let what will be, be,
I am so deeply smitten thro' the helm
That without help I cannot last till morn.
Thou therefore take my brand Excalibur,
Which was my pride: for thou rememberest how
In those old days, one summer noon, an arm

Rose up from out the bosom of the lake,
Clothed in white samite, mystic, wonderful,
Holding the sword – and how I row'd across
And took it, and have worn it, like a king:
And, wheresoever I am sung or told
In aftertime, this also shall be known:
But now delay not: take Excalibur,
And fling him far into the middle mere:
Watch what thou seëst, and lightly bring me word.'
    To him replied the bold Sir Bedivere:
'It is not meet, Sir King, to leave thee thus,
Aidless, alone, and smitten thro' the helm.
A little thing may harm a wounded man.
Yet I thy hest will all perform at full,
Watch what I see, and lightly bring thee word.'
    So saying, from the ruin'd shrine he stept
And in the moon athwart the place of tombs,
Where lay the mighty bones of ancient men,
Old knights, and over them the sea-wind sang
Shrill, chill, with flakes of foam. He, stepping down
By zig-zag paths, and juts of pointed rock,
Came on the shining levels of the lake.
    There drew he forth the brand Excalibur,
And o'er him, drawing it, the winter moon,
Brightening the skirts of a long cloud, ran forth
And sparkled keen with frost against the hilt:
For all the haft twinkled with diamond sparks,
Myriads of topaz-lights, and jacinth-work
Of subtlest jewellery. He gazed so long
That both his eyes were dazzled, as he stood,
This way and that dividing the swift mind,

In act to throw: but at the last it seem'd
Better to leave Excalibur conceal'd
There in the many-knotted waterflags,
That whistled stiff and dry about the marge.
So strode he back slow to the wounded King.

Then spake King Arthur to Sir Bedivere:
'Hast thou perform'd my mission which I gave?
What is it thou hast seen? or what hast heard?'

And answer made the bold Sir Bedivere:
'I heard the ripple washing in the reeds,
And the wild water lapping on the crag.'

To whom replied King Arthur, faint and pale:
'Thou hast betray'd thy nature and thy name,
Not rendering true answer, as beseem'd
Thy fëalty, nor like a noble knight:
For surer sign had follow'd, either hand,
Or voice, or else a motion of the mere.
This is a shameful thing for men to lie.
Yet now, I charge thee, quickly go again
As thou art lief and dear, and do the thing
I bad thee, watch, and lightly bring me word.'

Then went Sir Bedivere the second time
Across the ridge, and paced beside the mere,
Counting the dewy pebbles, fix'd in thought;
But when he saw the wonder of the hilt,
How curiously and strangely chased, he smote
His palms together, and he cried aloud,

'And if indeed I cast the brand away,
Surely a precious thing, one worthy note,
Should thus be lost for ever from the earth,
Which might have pleased the eyes of many men.

What good should follow this, if this were done?
What harm, undone? deep harm to disobey,
Seeing obedience is the bond of rule.
Were it well to obey then, if a king demand
An act unprofitable, against himself?
The King is sick, and knows not what he does.
What record, or what relic of my lord
Should be to aftertime, but empty breath
And rumours of a doubt? but were this kept,
Stored in some treasure-house of mighty kings,
Some one might show it at a joust of arms,
Saying, "King Arthur's sword, Excalibur,
Wrought by the lonely maiden of the Lake.
Nine years she wrought it, sitting in the deeps
Upon the hidden bases of the hills."
So might some old man speak in the aftertime
To all the people, winning reverence.
But now much honour and much fame were lost.'

  So spake he, clouded with his own conceit,
And hid Excalibur the second time,
And so strode back slow to the wounded King.

  Then spoke King Arthur, breathing heavily:
'What is it thou hast seen? or what hast heard?'

  And answer made the bold Sir Bedivere:
'I heard the water lapping on the crag,
And the long ripple washing in the reeds.'

  To whom replied King Arthur, much in wrath:
'Ah, miserable and unkind, untrue,
Unknightly, traitor-hearted! Woe is me!
Authority forgets a dying king,
Laid widow'd of the power in his eye

That bow'd the will. I see thee what thou art,
For thou, the latest-left of all my knights,
In whom should meet the offices of all,
Thou wouldst betray me for the precious hilt;
Either from lust of gold, or like a girl
Valuing the giddy pleasure of the eyes.
Yet, for a man may fail in duty twice,
And the third time may prosper, get thee hence:
But, if thou spare to fling Excalibur,
I will arise and slay thee with my hands.'
  Then quickly rose Sir Bedivere, and ran,
And, leaping down the ridges lightly, plunged
Among the bulrush-beds, and clutch'd the sword,
And strongly wheel'd and threw it. The great brand
Made lightnings in the splendour of the moon,
And flashing round and round, and whirl'd in anarch,
Shot like a streamer of the northern morn,
Seen where the moving isles of winter shock
By night, with noises of the northern sea.
So flash'd and fell the brand Excalibur:
But ere he dipt the surface, rose an arm
Clothed in white samite, mystic, wonderful,
And caught him by the hilt, and brandish'd him
Three times, and drew him under in the mere.
And lightly went the other to the King.
  Then spoke King Arthur, drawing thicker
   breath:
'Now see I by thine eyes that this is done.
Speak out: what is it thou hast heard, or seen?'
  And answer made the bold Sir Bedivere:
'Sir King, I closed mine eyelids, lest the gems

Should blind my purpose, for I never saw,
Nor shall see, here or elsewhere, till I die,
Not tho' I live three lives of mortal men,
So great a miracle as yonder hilt.
Then with both hands I flung him, wheeling him;
But when I look'd again, behold an arm,
Clothed in white samite, mystic, wonderful,
That caught him by the hilt, and brandish'd him
Three times, and drew him under in the mere.'

And answer made King Arthur, breathing hard:
'My end draws nigh; 'tis time that I were gone.
Make broad thy shoulders to receive my weight,
And bear me to the margin; yet I fear
My wound hath taken cold, and I shall die.'

So saying, from the pavement he half rose,
Slowly, with pain, reclining on his arm,
And looking wistfully with wide blue eyes
As in a picture. Him Sir Bedivere
Remorsefully regarded thro' his tears,
And would have spoken, but he found not words,
Then took with care, and kneeling on one knee,
O'er both his shoulders drew the languid hands,
And rising bore him thro' the place of tombs.

But, as he walk'd, King Arthur panted hard,
Like one that feels a nightmare on his bed
When all the house is mute. So sigh'd the King,
Muttering and murmuring at his ear, 'Quick, quick!
I fear it is too late, and I shall die.'
But the other swiftly strode from ridge to ridge,
Clothed with his breath, and looking, as he
        walk'd,

Larger than human on the frozen hills.
He heard the deep behind him, and a cry
Before. His own thought drove him, like a goad.
Dry clash'd his harness in the icy caves
And barren chasms, and all to left and right
The bare black cliff clang'd round him, as he based
His feet on juts of slippery crag that rang
Sharp-smitten with the dint of armed heels –
And on a sudden, lo! the level lake,
And the long glories of the winter moon.

Then saw they how there hove a dusky barge,
Dark as a funeral scarf from stem to stern,
Beneath them; and descending they were ware
That all the decks were dense with stately forms
Black-stoled, black-hooded, like a dream – by these
Three Queens with crowns of gold – and from
     them rose
A cry that shiver'd to the tingling stars,
And, as it were one voice an agony
Of lamentation, like a wind, that shrills
All night in a waste land, where no one comes,
Or hath come, since the making of the world.

Then murmur'd Arthur, 'Place me in the barge,'
And to the barge they came. There those three
     Queens
Put forth their hands, and took the King, and wept.
But she, that rose the tallest of them all
And fairest, laid his head upon her lap,
And loosed the shatter'd casque, and chafed his
     hands,
And call'd him by his name, complaining loud,

And dropping bitter tears against his brow
Striped with dark blood: for all his face was white
And colourless, and like the wither'd moon
Smote by the fresh beam of the springing east;
And all his greaves and cuisses dash'd with drops
Of onset; and the light and lustrous curls –
That made his forehead like a rising sun
High from the dïas-throne – were parch'd with
            dust;
Or, clotted into points and hanging loose,
Mix'd with the knightly growth that fringed his
            lips.
So like a shatter'd column lay the King;
Not like that Arthur who, with lance in rest,
From spur to plume a star of tournament,
Shot thro' the lists at Camelot, and charged
Before the eyes of ladies and of kings.

  Then loudly cried the bold Sir Bedivere,
'Ah! my Lord Arthur, whither shall I go?
Where shall I hide my forehead and my eyes?
For now I see the true old times are dead,
When every morning brought a noble chance,
And every chance brought out a noble knight.
Such times have been not since the light that led
The holy Elders with the gift of myrrh.
But now the whole ROUND TABLE is dissolved
Which was an image of the mighty world;
And I, the last, go forth companionless,
And the days darken round me, and the years,
Among new men, strange faces, other minds.'

  And slowly answered Arthur from the barge:

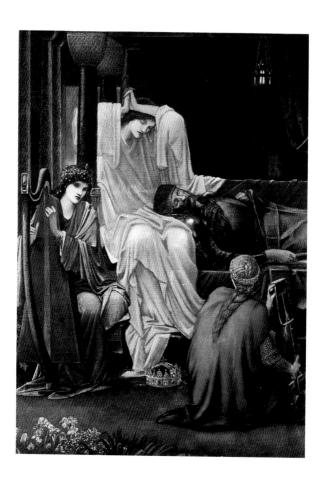

'The old order changeth, yielding place to new,
And God fulfils Himself in many ways,
Lest one good custom should corrupt the world.
Comfort thyself: what comfort is in me?
I have lived my life, and that which I have done
May He within Himself make pure! but thou,
If thou shouldst never see my face again,
Pray for my soul. More things are wrought by
     prayer
Than this world dreams of. Wherefore, let thy
     voice
Rise like a fountain for me night and day.
For what are men better than sheep or goats
That nourish a blind life within the brain,
If, knowing God, they lift not hands of prayer
Both for themselves and those who call them
     friend?
For so the whole round earth is every way
Bound by gold chains about the feet of God.
But now farewell. I am going a long way
With these thou seëst – if indeed I go –
(For all my mind is clouded with a doubt)
To the island-valley of Avilion;
Where falls not hail, or rain, or any snow,
Nor ever wind blows loudly; but it lies
Deep-meadow'd, happy, fair with orchard-lawns
And bowery hollows crown'd with summer sea,
Where I will heal me of my grievous wound.'

   So said he, and the barge with oar and sail
Moved from the brink, like some full-breasted
     swan.

From ULYSSES

There lies the port; the vessel puffs her sail:
There gloom the dark broad seas. My mariners,
Souls that have toil'd, and wrought, and thought
    with me –
That ever with a frolic welcome took
The thunder and the sunshine, and opposed
Free hearts, free foreheads – you and I are old;
Old age hath yet his honour and his toil;
Death closes all: but something ere the end,
Some work of noble note, may yet be done,
Not unbecoming men that strove with Gods.
The lights begin to twinkle from the rocks:
The long day wanes: the slow moon climbs: the deep
Moans round with many voices. Come, my friends,
'Tis not too late to seek a newer world.
Push off, and sitting well in order smite
The sounding furrows; for my purpose holds
To sail beyond the sunset, and the baths
Of all the western stars, until I die.
It may be that the gulfs will wash us down:
It may be we shall touch the Happy Isles,
And see the great Achilles, whom we knew.
Tho' much is taken, much abides; and tho'
We are not now that strength which in old days
Moved earth and heaven; that which we are, we are;
One equal temper of heroic hearts,
Made weak by time and fate, but strong in will
To strive, to seek, to find, and not to yield.

From
MAUD; A MONODRAMA

I

Come into the garden, Maud,
  For the black bat, night, has flown,
Come into the garden, Maud,
  I am here at the gate alone;
And the woodbine spices are wafted
    abroad,
    And the musk of the rose is blown.

II

For a breeze of morning moves,
  And the planet of Love is on high,
Beginning to faint in the light that she
    loves
  On a bed of daffodil sky,
To faint in the light of the sun she loves,
  To faint in his light, and to die.

III

All night have the roses heard
  The flute, violin, bassoon;
All night has the casement jessamine
    stirr'd
  To the dancers dancing in tune;
Till a silence fell with the waking bird,
  And a hush with the setting moon.

1X

Queen rose of the rosebud garden of girls,
 Come hither, the dances are done,
In gloss of satin and glimmer of pearls,
 Queen lily and rose in one;
Shine out, little head, sunning over with
  curls,
 To the flowers, and be their sun.

X

There has fallen a splendid tear
 From the passion-flower at the gate.
She is coming, my dove, my dear;
 She is coming, my life, my fate;
The red rose cries, 'She is near, she is near;'
 And the white rose weeps, 'She is late;'
The larkspur listens, 'I hear, I hear;'
 And the lily whispers, 'I wait.'

X1

She is coming, my own, my sweet;
 Were it ever so airy a tread,
My heart would hear her and beat,
 Were it earth in an earthy bed;
My dust would hear her and beat,
 Had I lain for a century dead;
Would start and tremble under her feet,
 And blossom in purple and red.

Break, Break, Break

Break, break, break,
   On thy cold gray stones, O Sea!
And I would that my tongue could utter
   The thoughts that arise in me.

O well for the fisherman's boy,
   That he shouts with his sister at play!
O well for the sailor lad,
   That he sings in his boat on the bay!

And the stately ships go on
   To their haven under the hill;
But O for the touch of a vanish'd hand,
   And the sound of a voice that is still!

Break, break, break,
   At the foot of thy crags, O sea!
But the tender grace of a day that is dead
   Will never come back to me.

Four songs from
THE PRINCESS

Sweet and low, sweet and low,
    Wind of the western sea,
Low, low, breathe and blow,
    Wind of the western sea!
Over the rolling waters go,
Come from the dying moon, and blow,
    Blow him again to me;
While my little one, while my pretty
      one, sleeps.

Sleep and rest, sleep and rest,
    Father will come to thee soon;
Rest, rest, on mother's breast,
    Father will come to thee soon;
Father will come to his babe in the nest,
Silver sails all out of the west
    Under the silver moon:
Sleep, my little one, sleep, my pretty
      one, sleep.

'Tears, idle tears, I know not what they
   mean,
Tears from the depth of some divine despair
Rise in the heart, and gather to the eyes,
In looking on the happy Autumn-fields,
And thinking of the days that are no more.

'Fresh as the first beam glittering on a sail,
That brings our friends up from the under-
   world,
Sad as the last which reddens over one
That sinks with all we love below the verge;
So sad, so fresh, the days that are no more.

'Ah, sad and strange as in dark summer
   dawns
The earliest pipe of half-awaken'd birds
To dying ears, when unto dying eyes
The casement slowly grows a glimmering
   square;
So sad, so strange, the days that are no more.

'Dear as remember'd kisses after death,
And sweet as those by hopeless fancy feign'd
On lips that are for others; deep as love,
Deep as first love, and wild with all regret;
O Death in Life, the days that are no more.'

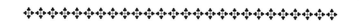

'Now sleeps the crimson petal, now the
    white;
Nor waves the cypress in the palace walk;
Nor winks the gold fin in the porphyry font:
The fire-fly wakens: waken thou with me.

   Now droops the milkwhite peacock like a
    ghost,
And like a ghost she glimmers on to me.

  Now lies the Earth all Danaë to the stars,
And all thy heart lies open unto me.

   Now slides the silent meteor on, and
    leaves
A shining furrow, as thy thoughts in me.

   Now folds the lily all her sweetness up,
And slips into the bosom of the lake:
So fold thyself, my dearest, thou, and slip
Into my bosom and be lost in me.'

The splendour falls on castle walls
    And snowy summits old in story:
The long light shakes across the lakes,
    And the wild cataract leaps in glory.
Blow, bugle, blow, set the wild echoes flying,
Blow, bugle; answer, echoes, dying, dying,
    dying.

O hark, O hear! how thin and clear,
    And thinner, clearer, farther going!
O sweet and far from cliff and scar
    The horns of Elfland faintly blowing!
Blow, let us hear the purple glens replying:
Blow, bugle; answer, echoes, dying, dying,
    dying.

O love, they die in yon rich sky,
    They faint on hill or field or river:
Our echoes roll from soul to soul,
    And grow for ever and for ever.
Blow, bugle, blow, set the wild echoes flying,
And answer, echoes, answer, dying, dying,
    dying.

The Charge of the Light Brigade

I

Half a league, half a league,
　Half a league onward,
All in the valley of Death
　Rode the six hundred.
'Forward, the Light Brigade!
Charge for the guns!' he said:
Into the valley of Death
　Rode the six hundred.

II

'Forward, the Light Brigade!'
Was there a man dismay'd?
Not tho' the soldier knew
　Some one had blunder'd:
Their's not to make reply,
Their's not to reason why,
Their's but to do and die:
Into the valley of Death
　Rode the six hundred.

III

Cannon to right of them,
Cannon to left of them,
Cannon in front of them
　Volley'd and thunder'd;
Storm'd at with shot and shell,
Boldly they rode and well,
Into the jaws of Death,
Into the mouth of Hell
　Rode the six hundred.

IV

Flash'd all their sabres bare,
Flash'd as they turn'd in air
Sabring the gunners there,
Charging an army, while
   All the world wonder'd:
Plunged in the battery-smoke
Right thro' the line they broke;
Cossack and Russian
Reel'd from the sabre-stroke
   Shatter'd and sunder'd.
Then they rode back, but not,
   Not the six hundred.

V

Cannon to right of them,
Cannon to left of them,
Cannon behind them
   Volley'd and thunder'd;
Storm'd at with shot and shell,
While horse and hero fell,
They that had fought so well
Came thro' the jaws of Death,
Back from the mouth of Hell,
All that was left of them,
   Left of six hundred.

VI

When can their glory fade?
O the wild charge they made!
   All the world wonder'd.
Honour the charge they made!
Honour the Light Brigade,
   Noble six hundred!

The Brook

I come from haunts of coot and hern,
  I make a sudden sally,
And sparkle out among the fern,
  To bicker down a valley.

By thirty hills I hurry down,
  Or slip between the ridges,
By twenty thorps, a little town,
  And half a hundred bridges.

Till last by Philip's farm I flow
  To join the brimming river,
For men may come and men may go
  But I go on for ever.

The Eagle

He clasps the crag with crooked hands;
Close to the sun in lonely lands,
Ring'd with the azure world, he stands.

The wrinkled sea beneath him crawls;
He watches from his mountain walls,
And like a thunderbolt he falls.

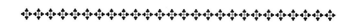

The Miller's Daughter

It is the miller's daughter,
    And she is grown so dear, so dear,
That I would be the jewel
    That trembles in her ear:
For hid in ringlets day and night,
I'd touch her neck so warm and white.

And I would be the girdle
    About her dainty dainty waist,
And her heart would beat against me,
    In sorrow and in rest:
And I should know if it beat right,
I'd clasp it round so close and tight.

And I would be the necklace,
    And all day long to fall and rise
Upon her balmy bosom,
    With her laughter or her sighs,
And I would lie so light, so light,
I scarce should be unclasp'd at night.

Six elegies from
IN MEMORIAM A.H.H.

VII

Dark house, by which once more I stand
 Here in the long unlovely street,
 Doors, where my heart was used to beat
So quickly, waiting for a hand,

A hand that can be clasp'd no more –
 Behold me, for I cannot sleep,
 And like a guilty thing I creep
At earliest morning to the door.

He is not here; but far away
 The noise of life begins again,
 And ghastly thro' the drizzling rain
On the bald street breaks the blank day.

LIV

Oh yet we trust that somehow good
   Will be the final goal of ill,
   To pangs of nature, sins of will,
Defects of doubt, and taints of blood;

That nothing walks with aimless feet;
   That not one life shall be destroy'd,
   Or cast as rubbish to the void,
When God hath made the pile complete;

That not a worm is cloven in vain;
   That not a moth with vain desire
   Is shrivell'd in a fruitless fire,
Or but subserves another's gain.

Behold, we know not anything;
   I can but trust that good shall fall
   At last – far off – at last, to all,
And every winter change to spring.

So runs my dream: but what am I?
   An infant crying in the night:
   An infant crying for the light:
And with no language but a cry.

LXVII

When on my bed the moonlight falls,
　　I know that in thy place of rest
　　By that broad water of the west,
There comes a glory on the walls:

Thy marble bright in dark appears,
　　As slowly steals a silver flame
　　Along the letters of thy name,
And o'er the number of thy years.

The mystic glory swims away;
　　From off my bed the moonlight dies;
　　And closing eaves of wearied eyes
I sleep till dusk is dipt in gray:

And then I know the mist is drawn
　　A lucid veil from coast to coast,
　　And in the dark church like a ghost
Thy tablet glimmers to the dawn.

CVI

Ring out, wild bells, to the wild sky,
    The flying cloud, the frosty light:
    The year is dying in the night;
Ring out, wild bells, and let him die.

Ring out the old, ring in the new,
    Ring, happy bells, across the snow:
    The year is going, let him go;
Ring out the false, ring in the true.

Ring out the grief that saps the mind,
    For those that here we see no more;
    Ring out the feud of rich and poor,
Ring in redress to all mankind.

Ring out a slowly dying cause,
    And ancient forms of party strife;
    Ring in the nobler modes of life,
With sweeter manners, purer laws.

Ring out the want, the care, the sin,
　　The faithless coldness of the times;
　　Ring out, ring out thy mournful rhymes,
But ring the fuller minstrel in.

Ring out false pride in place and blood,
　　The civic slander and the spite;
　　Ring in the love of truth and right,
Ring in the common love of good.

Ring out old shapes of foul disease;
　　Ring out the narrowing lust of gold;
　　Ring out the thousand wars of old,
Ring in the thousand years of peace.

Ring in the valiant man and free,
　　The larger heart, the kindlier hand;
　　Ring out the darkness of the land,
Ring in the Christ that is to be.

CXV

Now fades the last long streak of snow,
   Now burgeons every maze of quick
   About the flowering squares, and thick
By ashen roots the violets blow.

Now rings the woodland loud and long,
   The distance takes a lovelier hue,
   And drown'd in yonder living blue
The lark becomes a sightless song.

Now dance the lights on lawn and lea,
   The flocks are whiter down the vale,
   And milkier every milky sail
On winding stream or distant sea;

Where now the seamew pipes, or dives
   In yonder greening gleam, and fly
   The happy birds, that change their sky
To build and brood; that live their lives

From land to land; and in my breast
   Spring wakens too; and my regret
   Becomes an April violet,
And buds and blossoms like the rest.

CXXVI

Love is and was my Lord and King,
  And in his presence I attend
  To hear the tidings of my friend,
Which every hour his couriers bring.

Love is and was my King and Lord,
  And will be, tho' as yet I keep
  Within his court on earth, and sleep
Encompass'd by his faithful guard,

And hear at times a sentinel
  Who moves about from place to place,
  And whispers to the worlds of space,
In the deep night, that all is well.

Crossing the Bar

Sunset and evening star,
    And one clear call for me!
And may there be no moaning of the bar,
    When I put out to sea,

But such a tide as moving seems asleep,
    Too full for sound and foam,
When that which drew from out the bound-
      less deep
    Turns again home.

Twilight and evening bell,
    And after that the dark!
And may there be no sadness of farewell,
    When I embark;

For tho' from out our bourne of Time and
      Place
    The flood may bear me far,
I hope to see my Pilot face to face
    When I have crost the bar.

NOTES ON THE PICTURES

p. 6   *Tennyson Reading 'Maud'*, 1855, sketch by Dante Gabriel Rossetti (1828–1882). Birmingham Museums and Art Gallery.

p. 15   *The Lady of Shalott* (detail), 1888, by John William Waterhouse (1849–1917). Tate Gallery, London.

p. 18   *The Lotus Eaters*, photogravure by William Edward Frank Britten (*op.* 1873–1888). From *The Early Poems of Alfred Lord Tennyson*, Methuen and Co.,1901.

p. 27   *Bedivere throws Excalibur into the Lake*, illustration from a thirteenth-century French manuscript *Roman de Lancelot*. British Library, London. Photo: Bridgeman Art Library, London.

p. 31   *The Last Sleep of Arthur in Avalon* (detail), 1881–1898, by Sir Edward Burne-Jones (1833–1898). Museo de Arte, Ponce, Puerto Rico. Photo: Bridgeman Art Library, London.

p. 34   *April Love*, 1855–1856, by Arthur Hughes (1832–1915). Tate Gallery, London. Photo: Bridgeman Art Library, London.

p. 39   *Shepherd's Cottage* (detail) by Thomas McEwan (1846–1914). Smith Art Gallery and Museum, Stirling. Photo: Bridgeman Art Library, London.

p. 42   *Bamburgh Castle, Northumberland* by Thomas Girton (1775–1802). Tate Gallery, London. Photo: Bridgeman Art Library, London.

p. 46   *Waterfall on the River Neath, South Wales* by James Burrell Smith (*op.* 1850–1881). Roy Miles Gallery, London. Photo: Bridgeman Art Library, London.

p. 51   *Landscape at Night* (detail) by Nathan Theodore Fielding (*op.* 1775–1818). University of Liverpool Art Gallery and Collections. Photo: Bridgeman Art Library, London.

p. 55   *Arthur Henry Hallam*, c. 1832, by James Spedding (1808–1881). Lincolnshire Library Service.

p. 59   *Near Harlech, North Wales* (detail) by Benjamin Williams Leader (1831–1923). Christie's, London. Photo: Bridgeman Art Library, London.

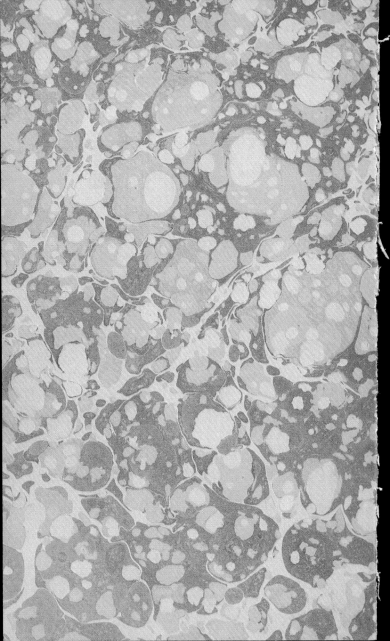